MW00933919

IN TIME

THE
**AMAZING
RACE**

Issue 4/ December 2023

Unlock the secrets to victory with this magazine! Packed with rules, fun facts, and essential information to make your race successful...

2nd Annual Amazing MLP Scavenger Hunt

Race against the other teams to be the first to finish. This race has 5 stages which can be done in any order. At each stage you will chose one of two tasks to complete. You may complete either task and you may switch tasks at any time.

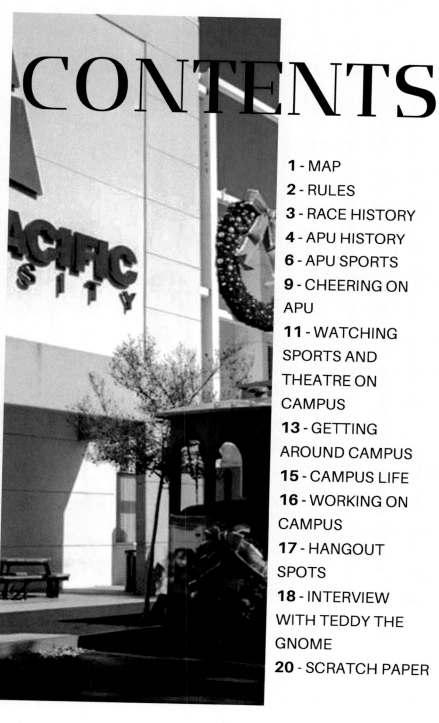

CONTENTS

Azusa Pacific University East Campus

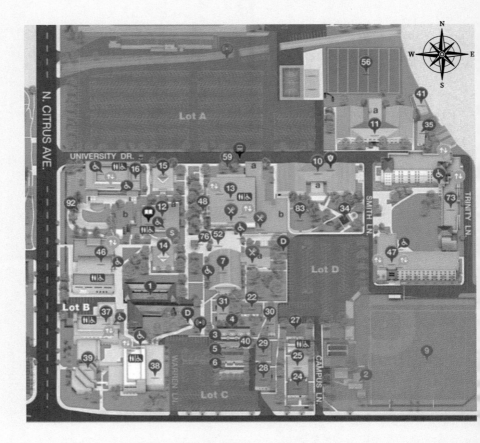

All red shaded areas are out of bounds. Remember no part of this race is on the West campus.

RULES

General Info
- The race has 5 stages. You may complete the stages in **any order**.
- Complete one task at each stage. Note there are 2 tasks available for each stage. Choose either task.
- When you arrive at a stage, check in with the teacher or APU representative. At that time they will tell you what page in your race book to complete.
- You can switch tasks at any time. (Hint- if you do not know how to do the task there is a good chance the other task will have less complicated math).
- A stage is only complete once you present a correct answer or complete the requirements and the teacher or APU representative stamps the stage in your race book.
- Once you complete all 5 stages, return to the starting room in TCC (Building 10) to end your time.

Going from Location to Location
- No task will start inside a building. Remember that classes are going on. Finals are NEXT WEEK.
- You may NOT walk through any parking lots. DO NOT walk in the middle of the road.
- **NO part of this race takes place on West campus. You may not get on the trolly.**

Bonuses
- Bonuses are in the back of your race book. All bonuses help decrease your overall time.
- You may not complete any additional bonuses once your check in at the end of the race.

This is the 4th Scavenger Hunt MPASS Education has hosted.

The AVHSD teachers participated in the first ever Amazing Scavenger Hunt which was held in San Diego in June 2022. The first student version of The Amazing MLP Scavenger Hunt was held at UCLA in October 2022. There are several students racing today who participated in last years race. Although they have more experience, each year the race platform, questions, and location changes. The winning team from Littlerock High School all graduated last May.

Every race we have found new ways to make the race logistically smoother. From texting pictures to the hosts to this year having a race book for each team.

APU HISTORY

OVERVIEW

Azusa Pacific University, one of the largest Christian universities in the US, began on March 3, 1899, when a group of women and men passionate about creating a place for Christian education gathered to form the Training School for Christian Workers. APU was the first Bible college on the West Coast geared toward preparing men and women for ministry and service. Meeting in a home in Whittier, California, led by President Mary A. Hill, the school grew to an enrollment of 12 in its first term.

In the early years the school relocated and changed leadership several times. The university relocated to Azusa in 1946.

LEADER IN CHRISTIAN HIGHER EDUCATION

Today, APU offers 71 bachelor's degrees, 44 master's degrees, 25 certificates, 8 credentials, and 9 doctoral programs. The university holds accreditation from the WASC Senior College and University Commission as well as 14 other specialized accreditations.

Presidents

In July 2022, APU welcomed its 18th president, Adam J. Morris, PhD. Having received unanimous support from the board, Morris is a nationally recognized and accomplished senior administrator and lifelong advocate for Christian higher education.

Many universities have blazed a new trail in recent decades with their first female president. Unlike most universities Azusa's first 4 presidents were women.

1. Mary A. Hill: 1900 - 1901
2. Anna Draper: 1901 - 1903
3. Bertha Pinkham Dixon: 1903 - 1904
4. Matilda Atkinson: 1904 - 1909
5. William P. Pinkham: 1909 - 1919
6. Eli Reece: 1919 - 1923
7. Lowell H. Coate: 1923 - 1924
8. George A. McLaughlin: 1924 - 1927
9. Ray L. Carter: 1927 - 1931
10. David H. Scott: 1931 - 1936
11. B.C. Johnson: 1936 - 1937
12. William Kirby: 1937-1939
13. Cornelius P. Haggard: 1939 - 1975
14. Paul E. Sago: 1976 - 1989
15. Richard E. Felix: 1990 - 2000
16. Jon R. Wallace: 2000 - 2019
17. Paul W. Ferguson: 2019 - 2021

APU SPORTS

The university's award-winning athletics program consists of 18 teams. Before becoming a member of the NCAA Division II in fall 2012, Cougar Athletics won an unprecedented eight consecutive NAIA Directors' Cup awards. APU belongs to the Pacific West Conference except for women's water polo (in GCC); women's swimming and diving, (in PCSC); and women's acrobatics and tumbling, (in NCATA).

Since joining the PacWest, Azusa Pacific has captured 46 conference titles and counting. Since their entry into the NCAA Division II level, the Cougars have also captured two National titles, both in Women's Track and Field in 2021 and 2023. Mens and Womens Track and Field have both won 7 titles in a row.

#ONEBLOODFOOTBALL

FOOTBALL COMES TO A CLOSE

In December 2020, after a significant review and careful consideration, Azusa Pacific University ended its inter football program after 55 years of competition in the NCAA and NAIA. The decision did not come lightly, but was made due to the decline in collegiate football in California.

APU BASEBALL

Baseball is one of the 2 facilities on East Campus. Most sports (including the Athletics Department) are located on West Campus.

Like many of their counterparts in higher education and the professional sphere, the baseball team boasts a plethora of jersey selections. Options include 3 jerseys (Black, Brick, & Striped), 2 pants (Grey and White), and 3 hats (Black, Brick, and Black with red logo and bill).

PACK THE HOUSE

APU Baseball Stadium is on the smaller side for baseball stadiums . They have 2 sets of bleachers. The larger bleacher has 9 rows and is 48 feet long.

The smaller bleacher, behind home plate, has 5 rows that are each 30 feet long. To calculate seating capacity, use a standard of 16 inch width per person. APU is considering adding an additional set of bleachers to increase total capacity.

Looking Your Best

in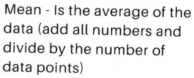

All sports have numerous statistics. On Base Percentage (OBP) in baseball, and Field Goal Percentage (FG%) in Basketball are two of the most common. Generally sports stats are shown in a box score. Strategically select which stats to highlight when trying to make the team or individual look their best.

Must Have Stats

The most commonly used basic statistics include mean, median, and mode.

Mean - Is the average of the data (add all numbers and divide by the number of data points)
Median - Is the middle value of the data when listed in order.
Mode - The data value that appears the most often

Cheering on APU

FIGHT SONG

For His honor, APU.
Always faithful, ever true.
In every challenge, every test,
offer your very best.
Fight the good fight, persevere.
Onward, upward, victory is near.
Let every day bring faith anew.
Honor Him, APU.

CHEER!!

One of the most common ways to support athletic teams is through cheerleaders. Dancing and chanting for the team and crowd. Some cheers are very compicated and long with many steps and verses. Others are quite short so everyone in the crowd can join in.

COUGARS

In 1965, the students were put to the task of selecting a mascot. It was said that cougars were known to roam the San Gabriel Mountains, so it was only natural that students decided to pay tribute to the rumored mountainside dwellers. The mascot today, known amongst students as the Coug, is an active participant in athletic and campus-life events.

REP THE SWAG

Most colleges sell spirit-wear to increase revenue. Fans buy shirts and other swag to show their support. Remember, that selling items is intended to make money. When designing products one must try to keep production costs low to help increase profits. Some ways to decrease production cost is to buy in bulk, limit the number of print colors and print locations and type of material.

Recently Azusa purchased 1500 shirts (exactly like the one the mascot is wearing in page 9). Each shirt costs $8 to make and APU bookstore will sell it for $15 each. They are concerned that they may not make their money back since the purchased all the shirts up front.

WATCHING SPORTS AND THEATRE ON CAMPUS

COST FOR SPORTS

Volleyball, Men's & Women's Tennis, Swimming & Diving, Baseball, Softball, Acrobatics & Tumbling, Cross Country, and Water Polo are free for all in attendance. Men's and Women's Basketball is $12 for Adults, but free for APU students (with student ID). Soccer costs $7 for Adults, but is free for APU Students.

THEATRE

APU theatre department usually puts on 4 productions per academic year. For the 2023-2024 school year the plays are *Rodgers & Hammerstein's Cinderella, Murder on the Orient Express, Much Ado About Nothing,* and *Silent Sky.* Most productions run for about 2 weeks with shows on Thursdays, Fridays and 2 on Saturdays, for a total of 8-10 shows. All productions are at either the Warehouse Theater or the Blackbox Theatre, both of which are on West Campus.

Theater Ticket Prices

The theatre department sells both single show tickets as well as a season pass. The prices are outlined below.

GENERAL TICKET PRICES

General Admission - $21
Students - $18
Children 12 and under - $18
Seniors - $18
APU Students (with ID) - $17

Season Tickets

With a season ticket you get entry into each of the plays 1 time.

General Admission - $70
Students - $70
Children 12 and under - $70
Seniors - $70
APU Students (with ID) - $65

Getting Around Campus

Walking

The most common way for students to get round East Campus is by walking. Almost everyone has a slightly different walking rate, the average college student's walking rate is 18 minutes per mile. Most students know how long it takes to get from one building to another through repetition. Another way to find the time it takes to walk from one place to another is to calculate your average walking rate. To determine your average walking rate, walk a set distance 5 times, then calculate the average. Once you know your walking rate, apply that to the total distance of the route. For example, if my average walking rate going 100 feet is 20 seconds, then it takes 80 seconds to walk 400 feet (20 x 4 = 80 and 100 x 4 = 400). This method only works if you maintain a steady pace.

Accessability

As with any campus (public or private) the question of accessibility is often brought up. The most common way to make buildings accessible is through the use of ramps and automatic doors. One problem is not all ramps are created equal. For a ramp to be marked as ADA accessible, the ramp must have a slope of 1:12 (in inches) or about 5 degrees of incline or less.

THE TROLLY

** You may NOT get on the trolly at any time.

Transportation Services utilizes trollys and buses to shuttle people between East and West campuses from 6:45 a.m. – 11 p.m. Monday through Friday during normal class sessions.

Monday through Thursday there is one trolly that runs continuously. It takes 6 minutes to get from East Campus to West Campus. There are 3 stops on West Campus. A trolly arrives at the east stop on average every 20 minutes.

Campus Life

Azusa Pacific has 3 Resident Halls on campus (Adams, Engstrom, & Trinity). The dorms cost $2,887 per semester. Each semester contract is for 4 months. When staying in a dorm you must purchase meal plan C at the minimum. Meal plans are provided in the table.

Meal Plans

	Cost per semester
Cougar Plan A: 20 weekly meals and $175 flex	$2,700
Cougar Plan B: 15 weekly meals and $175 flex	$2,450
Cougar Plan C: 12 weekly meals and $150 flex	$1,975
Cougar Plan D: 9 weekly meals and $100 flex	$1,500
Cougar Plan E: 3 weekly meals and $350 flex	$830
Cougar Plan F: 0 weekly meals and $400 flex	$400

Not all students want to, or have the means to live on campus. Azusa Pacific has a large population of commuter students. Many of which live with their parents to save money. Commuter students need to purchase a parking pass for $150 per semester. We talked to Jacob about his commute. He attends classes 5 days a week and lives 6.7 miles away. His car gets 20 miles per gallon and has a 15 gallon gas tank. He was mentioning that with the price of gas averaging $5.05 in California, he may not be saving too much money.

Work Life *at* APU

Searching for a student employment position at APU is similar to obtaining employment with other organizations. The Office of Student Employment can offer guidance throughout the process and will ensure that all hire-related documentation is obtained and accurate in accordance with California and federal employment law and practice through their onboarding system.

It is suggested that full time college students work a maximum of 20 hours per week. This will help students balance work and school. At APU student employees are limited to 29 hours per week.

APU students generally earn minimum wage, which is $16 per hour (starting Jan. 1 2024). Students can make as much as $21 per hour without getting board approval but that is very rare, and takes a long time.

Hangout Spots
ON EAST CAMPUS

Discovering the Hidden Gem of the 7 Palms

Seven Palms is one of the student body's favorite spots to soak up some sun. A small grass amphitheater with 7 huge palm trees along one side. This amphitheater is used for spoken word and movie nights.

Exploring the Wynn Amphitheater

This venue provides a study space in a beautiful, open-air atmosphere, while also serving as a location for large groups to gather and listen to speakers or music groups. The grassy area between the steps and seating area have artificial turf. The grassy area around the stage is difficult to maintain. Turf cost $11 per square foot.

Interview with a Gnome

As smartphones steal the show, toys have to get creative for some thrills. That's where bungee jumping comes in! Lately, it seems like every toy is taking the plunge.

After chasing Teddy the Gnome between his epic jumps, we finally caught up with him and asked the burning question: Why did he and his crew start this wild adventure? Without a moment's hesitation, he pointed a tiny finger and blamed the phones for it all! Apparently, they're behind the decline of good old-fashioned toy playtime.

So now, toys everywhere are just aimlessly wandering around, trying to find ways to pass the time.

When quizzed on the crew's favorite jumping spot, he quipped, "Anywhere with a thrill!"

We went all out to squeeze every bit of info from him. After some digging, we learned that his buddies usually chicken out at 20 feet. We asked why, and he snickered, "Well, if you were a teeny-weeny 6 inches tall, 20 feet would feel like a whopping 100!"

Check out their next jump December 5, 2023 at APU off the rail of TCC. This is not their highest jump but is close at 19 feet.

" Anywhere with a thrill "

Teddy has a 14 person jump crew. They have jumped so often that all of them have an equation to more easily know how to safely jump from any height. In each equation y represents the fall height in inches and x represents the number of rubber bands. Its not too crazy as almost everyone in his crew has at least one friend that uses the same equation.

Teddy
$y = 12x + 5$
$R^2 = 0.82$

Sock Monkeys
$y = 5x + 3$
$R^2 = 0.98$

Unicorns
$y = 10x + 13$
$R^2 = 0.83$

Red Gnomes
$y = 11x + 4$
$R^2 = 0.85$

Food Stuffies
$y = 5x + 4$
$R^2 = 0.99$

Puppies
$y = 6x + 9$
$R^2 = 0.87$

Scratch Paper

Use this page and the next as scratch paper as needed for calculations, planning, or drawing diagrams.

Scratch Paper

The Amazing MLP Scavenger Hunt 2023

This event was created by MPASS Education for the purpose of encouraging high school students to apply mathematics in real world context as well as demonstrate the characteristics of math literacy which include, communication, collaboration, critical thinking, productive failure, problem solving, and perseverance. Additionally, this event provides an opportunity for students to gain success experiences on a college campus.

MPASS Education wants to thank our host, Azusa Pacific University for their collaboration and support of this event. We also want to thank the teachers and administrators of Antelope Valley Union High School District for supporting their students prepare and compete in this event.

Made in the USA
Las Vegas, NV
25 November 2023

81470537R00017